145 MILLION YEARS AGO   65.5 MILLION YEARS AGO

C R E T A C E O U S

- climate moist and cooler

- continents fully formed by end
  of the period; expanded coasts,
  widened oceans

- flowering plants spread,
  completely changing the
  landscape

- creatures flourish and diversify:
  sea life, birds, small mammals,
  frogs, turtles, etc.

- dinosaurs rule the earth

- Cretaceous ends with a mass
  extinction (due to asteroid?) and
  dinosaurs killed off

How do we know what dinosaurs really looked like?

SCALY SPOTTED
FEATHERED FRILLED

By the Sibert medalist **CATHERINE THIMMESH**

HOUGHTON MIFFLIN HARCOURT
Boston New York

The text of this book is set in Din.

Library of Congress Cataloging-in-Publication Data
Thimmesh, Catherine.
Scaly spotted feathered frilled : how do we know what dinosaurs really looked like? / by Catherine
Thimmesh.
    pages cm
Audience: Grade 4 and up.
ISBN 978-0-547-99134-4
1. Dinosaurs—Juvenile literature. 2. Paleoart—Juvenile literature. 3. Paleontology—Juvenile literature.
I. Title.
 QE861.5.T475 2013
 567.9—dc23
  2012048466

Manufactured in China
SCP 10 9 8 7 6 5 4 3 2 1
4500421881

DINOSAURS THUNDER ACROSS THE SILVER screen at the movies.

They snarl and snap and stare menacingly from the pages of many a great book.

Their enormous bones tower majestically in museum halls.

And yet, no one has ever laid eyes on a *real* dinosaur before. After all, they lived more than sixty-five million years ago. Long, *long* before people were around.

We have no photographs capturing their toothy grins; no ancient sculptures carved from their likenesses; no cave paintings detailing those fantastical frills.

So . . . how do we know what dinosaurs really looked like?

"*Until we see one walking through the door, or we build a time machine to go back, dinosaur reconstruction will always be a certain amount of guesswork. But it's guesswork based on science,*" says John Sibbick, a world-renowned paleoartist.

Recreating dinosaurs is like putting together a three-dimensional jigsaw puzzle—with plenty of pieces missing. The challenge falls to the many different paleoscientists and paleoartists—specialists in the prehistoric world, and puzzle-masters, all of them.

To begin with, they need dinosaur bones: deeply snuggled in layer upon layer of rock, where they slowly—ever so slowly—become fossils. Until, one day, with lots of luck, the fossil bones are discovered by paleontologists (or by amateur fossil hunters).

Next, the scientists tackle questions and hunt for answers. Paleontologists study the fossils in detail: *What kind of dinosaur is it?* Geologists study the rocks where the fossils were found: *How old are the fossils? What do they reveal about the habitat of the dinosaur?* Paleobotanists study the plant life of the time: *What did the dinosaur eat? How did it live?*

© Greg Paul. These three dinosaurs, *Albertosaurus*, *Anchiceratops*, and *Hypacrosaurus* (from left to right), flourished in the late Cretaceous period. Greg Paul based his restoration on several known fossil skeletons and skulls from each of these dinosaurs, as well as skin impressions (and some mummies of *Hypacrosaurus*). The habitat of these animals is known to have been forested coastal swamps and marshes, and thus the artist incorporated this habitat into the image. (See page 33 for another *Anchiceratops*.)

5

Gregory Paul 79

Finally, the paleoartists (who are often scientists as well) attempt to create an image—a picture of what the dinosaur might have looked like.

Whereas many illustrators depict dinosaurs for entertainment and draw from their imagination, paleoartists draw first from scientific evidence. Their goal is to create the most accurate representation possible, not the most dramatic.

"Whether it's a well-known dinosaur or not, I surround myself with all the information," explains renowned paleoartist Mark Hallett. *"I come to my own conclusions, and I don't trust secondhand interpretations. I absorb everything I can, and then I start by sketching the known."*

Paleoartists use the fossil bones, and the plant studies, and the rock studies, and all of the other bits of evidence discovered by the various scientists. Then they attempt to bridge the divide between the "knowns" and the "unknowns."

© Mark Hallett. *Seismosaurus* is known only from a single skeleton. Mark Hallett drew these sauropods in their habitat, which was known to be semiarid with open floodplains. Based on trackway evidence (see pages 16–17), several types of sauropods are known to have traveled in herds as the artist depicted here—however, it is unknown if this particular species of sauropod traveled that way, since only one skeleton has been found so far.

"*Scientific research really drives the visual image,*" explains Sylvia Czerkas, one half of the famed Czerkas paleoart team. "*It's very important for us to start with the science and then put into the image what we've learned.*"

Studying the fossils and plants and rocks helps the paleoartists answer many critical questions:

Did dinosaurs drag or lift their tails?

Did they or didn't they have lizard-like scales? Or even feathers?

Did they lumber slowly or zip around at top speeds?

Because although a fossil is not a time machine, it is a window—cracked open ever so slightly—into the deep past.

© John Sibbick. John Sibbick based this art on fossil finds of three skeletons of *Scelidosaurus*—a fairly complete adult and two fragmentary (possible) juveniles—found on the Dorset coast in the United Kingdom. The sketch (below) was Sibbick's last stage in working out the dinosaur shape and the layout of the armored scutes (bony scales). The finished scene (right) shows how the group may have met their end during a tsunami event.

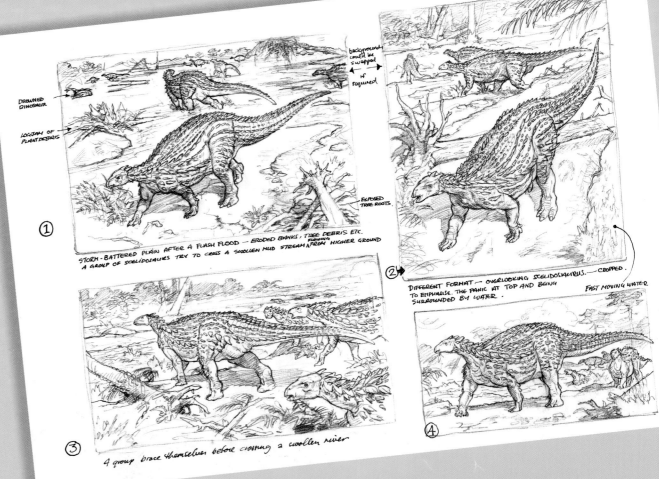

① STORM-BATTERED PLAIN AFTER A FLASH FLOOD — ERODED BANKS, TREE DEBRIS ETC.
A GROUP OF SCELIDOSAURS TRY TO CROSS A SWOLLEN MUD STREAM FLOWING FROM HIGHER GROUND

② DIFFERENT FORMAT — OVERLOOKING SCELIDOSAURUS. CROPPED.
TO EMPHASISE. THE PANIC AT TOP AND BEING SURROUNDED BY WATER.

FAST MOVING WATER

③ A group brace themselves before crossing a swollen river

DROWNED DINOSAUR

LOGJAM OF PLANT DEBRIS

EXPOSED TREE ROOTS.

background could be swapped if required

1

2

UNLIKE ANYTHING EVER SEEN BEFORE

WHEN SCIENTISTS AND ARTISTS FIRST began peering into the deep past using the few fossils they had, what little they could see was understandably muddled.

But that didn't stop them from trying to recreate these creatures. Thirty years after the first dinosaur fossils were found in England, sculptor Benjamin Waterhouse Hawkins created the first life-sized dinosaurs and unveiled them to an eager public in the 1850s (at the Crystal Palace in London). They were unlike anything ever seen before.

The sculptures were alien-like—and mind-boggling and amazing—and the people who saw them were awestruck. Never mind that in hindsight the dinosaurs weren't particularly accurate.

Waterhouse's image of *Iguanodon,* for example, was based on only a few fossil bones and some teeth. Since the teeth were remarkably similar to a modern-day iguana's (thus the species name), and since there was little else to go on, Waterhouse essentially sculpted a very large, modified iguana.

© National History Museum, London. Benjamin Waterhouse Hawkins's sketch for his dinosaur sculptures for the 1850s exhibit at the Crystal Palace in London. This shows *Iguanodon* standing in the back. Notice the small horn on its nose. Later, scientists discovered it was really a spike belonging on the thumb. (See page 17 for a modern view of *Iguanodon.*)

Still, he got some things right: *Iguanodons* (and dinosaurs in general) *did* stand on straight legs, unlike their belly-dragging reptilian relatives.

Waterhouse's images ignited the public's fascination with dinosaurs, and paleontologists and fossil hunters responded to the enthusiasm by digging for—and finding—more and more bones.

And so by the 1890s, with more evidence to work from, artists had ushered in a new era of understanding and accuracy through their art. Charles R. Knight, considered the best paleoartist of his day, popularized the dinosaur image. His dinosaurs were less alien-like and more believable inhabitants of the natural world. Still, scientists today consider most dinosaur depictions from that time to be outdated.

That "old" look of the dinosaurs stemmed from the limited fossil evidence and a limited understanding of evolution. Not to mention the prevailing theories of the time: particularly that dinosaurs were cold-blooded and small-brained, like lizards—sluggish, with tails dragging.

This interpretation defined dinosaurs for a hundred years or so. Then, during the Great Depression and World War II (1920s–40s), dinosaur research—from new fossil discoveries to field studies to art restorations— came to a virtual standstill.

But dinosaur science came roaring back in the 1960s, and by 1975 there was a seismic shakeup in how dinosaurs were viewed.

The conventional wisdom was flipped upside down: cold became warm; slow became fast; upright posture became horizontal.

In 1975, paleontologist Robert Bakker argued that dinosaurs were not sluggish, tail-dragging, cold-blooded, lizard-like beasts but were really warm-blooded, active creatures.

He made the case that most dinosaurs could sustain high activity levels and regulate their own body temperature. He presented compelling evidence and analysis for his theories . . . and instantly ignited a great scientific brouhaha.

Perhaps one of the best pieces of evidence supporting the warm-blooded theory was also one of the greatest dinosaur discoveries of all time. Paleontologist John Ostrom (a teacher of Bakker's) discovered the first specimen of *Deinonychus* in 1964—on the very last day of his expedition, on his way back to the camp. Most extraordinary was the dino's claw—which came not from the arm, as might be expected, but rather from the foot! In order for the dinosaur to use the claw while attacking, it would have to *balance* on one foot. Balance and hop around on one foot! While fighting! Certainly an active, warm-blooded creature!

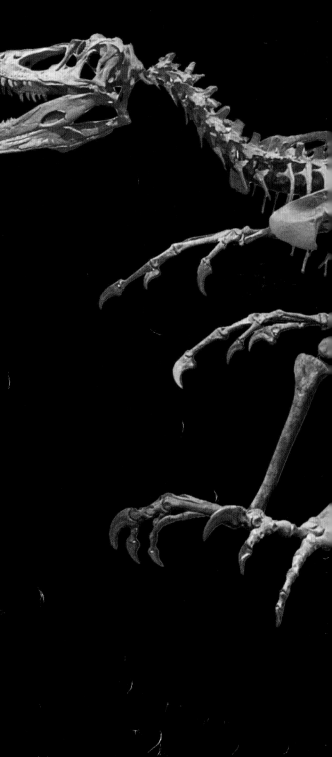

Today, most (but not all) scientists and paleoartists agree—based on the abundance of supporting evidence—that the dinosaurs were in fact warm-blooded. And remarkably, the dinosaur's own footprints point in that direction.

THEY'RE MOVING FAST

AROUND THE WORLD—ON EVERY CONTINENT except Antarctica—scientists have discovered millions of dinosaur trackways. These are pathways of uninterrupted dinosaur footprints—preserved as fossils in the sediment. Thousands of them have been mapped, measured, and analyzed.

"It's not just the odd footprint," explains John Sibbick. "These trackways are a continuous trail of dinosaurs. The tracks . . . they don't cross over, they run parallel; so it's a good inference the dinosaurs were traveling together."

These trackways are ancient snapshots of actual dinosaur activity—a concrete record of a given moment in time. They give the paleoartist a glimpse at millions-of-years-old life in motion—and provide more support for behavioral theories; more clues on dinosaurs' gait and posture, agility and speed.

"And the trackways backed it all up," enthuses John Sibbick. "You find the trackways and they're moving fast—migrating to where the food is and away from predators. It's unbelievable in some cases how mobile they were."

Trackways provide plenty of answers, including how various dinosaur species stood and walked; whether they were bipedal (walked on two legs) or quadrupedal (walked on all fours); whether they traveled in a herd or a pack; what types of species lived in a particular region; and the speed at which the dinosaur was traveling.

© John Sibbick. This scene of *Iguanodons* walking along the shoreline of the Cretaceous-era seaway shows three adults and three juveniles (or smaller females) leaving parallel sequences of tracks. The scene is based on fossilized track marks found in Colorado, sometimes dubbed the Dinosaur Freeway. The trackways clearly show these dinosaurs were quadrupedal (walked on all fours), and the scene implies they traveled as a structured group. (See page 10 for "old" view.)

Trackways also corrected some popular misconceptions.

"Out of thousands of dinosaur trackways," explains preeminent paleoartist Greg Paul, *"only a handful show tail drag marks. This firmly establishes the hypothesis that all dinosaurs carried their tails off the ground."*

Not only do the trackways confirm that tails were carried off the ground—which affected the overall structure and posture of the skeleton—but the trackways also bolstered the warm-blooded hypothesis. With tails lifted, these dinos could move!

This "new" look—sleek and anatomically correct, with a horizontal posture and a lifted tail—reflects a deeper and better understanding of dinosaur biology, thanks to an ever-increasing pile of fossil evidence.

In addition to the trackway evidence, scientists made other exciting discoveries: dino nesting grounds (mothers who took care of their eggs); evidence of mass migration (shown in the trackways); and polar habitats (also supporting the warm-blooded theory, since cold-blooded creatures need warm weather to survive).

Scientists also developed new and better technologies: CT scanners to peer deep inside bones; high-resolution x-rays to identify fossils hidden in stone; 3D laser scanners to capture a digital record of the fossil; microscopic and molecular studies to examine the fossil at the cellular level; and advanced computer technologies to determine, for example, the range of motion of a dinosaur's neck.

"Dinosaurs are a group of 'exotic' animals whose biology is not obvious from the start, unlike fossil mammals or lizards," explains Greg Paul. *"It has taken time to build up the knowledge base needed to resolve their true form and nature."*

ABOVE: © National Museum of Natural History, Smithsonian Institution. Charles R. Knight, artist. *Triceratops*. 1901. (See page 24 for skeletal mount.)

OPPOSITE: © Mark Hallett. Painted nearly a hundred years after Knight's image above, Hallett's art shows two male *Triceratops* in conflict over territory and mating rights and reflects the current understanding of this dinosaur.

Several differences between Knight's image and Hallett's are immediately identifiable:

a) The skin pattern and texture in Hallett's painting reflects the discoveries of skin impressions from earlier in the 1980s. These discoveries showed skin with repeating patterns of large, flattened scales with polygonal sides. The larger scale was surrounded by smaller, similar scales, and the entire pattern was made up of scales that did not overlap.

b) The triangular bones on the margins of the *Triceratops*'s frill didn't always get preserved, which may be why Knight didn't show them.

c) Hallett's version reflects the warm-blooded dinosaur theory of the 1970s, showing highly active dinosaurs.

d) The correct stance of the forelimb (front leg) of *Triceratops* has always been contentious: Is it splayed out or straight under the body? Trackways and imaging studies have shown it is somewhere in between.

PREVIOUS PAGE: © Greg Paul. Daspletosaurus. *Greg Paul has heavily modified this image from his original. In addition to changing forested background to a cattail marsh to better represent the presumed habitat, the artist improved the profile of the dinosaur based on a more rigorous skeletal restoration.*

THE SKELETON GIVES OVERALL DIMENSIONS

"**Y**OU'RE LUCKY TO FIND ANYTHING, *actually,*" *says John Sibbick. "It's almost a miracle when anything is left, because of scavengers, weather, and just a lack of suitable conditions for fossilization."*

When dinosaurs were first discovered in England in the 1820s, the recovered fossils numbered only a couple of teeth and a handful of bones. Not much for an artist to work with.

But now, there is more.

Over seven hundred dinosaur species are known and named—and that number continues to grow. Many of the species are represented by several specimens, or individuals; and many of them are represented by at least fifty percent of a recovered skeleton or skull.

With more bones in the record, scientists generally achieve greater accuracy when putting them together. But sometimes, even if put together correctly, scientists occasionally misidentify a dinosaur.

Brontosaurus, the biggest, baddest dinosaur at the time of its discovery, immediately became a sensation with the public—despite some hidden problems. For one thing, the nearly complete skeleton lacked a skull. Unfortunately, paleontologists gave *Brontosaurus* a skull that was the wrong shape and size.

© American Museum of Natural History. Charles R. Knight's *Brontosaurus.* In addition to showing the wrong head (a large, robust skull like *Camarasaurus,* rather than a correct, smaller skull like *Diplodocus*), this image portrays an incorrect lifestyle. No *Brontosaurus/Apatosaurus* dinosaurs have been discovered in ancient waterbeds. Their feet are not suited for walking through marsh. Studies have shown *Apatosaurus* was in fact a land-dwelling creature.

Most unfortunate of all, *Brontosaurus* was not the first and only known specimen of his species (as originally thought), but was actually an adult version of *Apatosaurus* (who was known only from juvenile specimens). And since *Apatosaurus* had been discovered and named first, that species name took precedence. *Brontosaurus* eventually got a new (and proper) head, and a correct new name—*Apatosaurus.*

Misidentification is one problem—but what really makes dinosaur reconstruction such an enormous challenge, is that finding a complete skeleton is exceptionally rare.

Luckily, though, a couple of things help an artist. First, a skeleton is a mirror image of itself: right side matching left side. Second, several specimens of the same dinosaur species can be combined to help fill in the gaps.

Most times, such a composite skeleton—a single dinosaur formed from several individuals (a leg bone here, a hip bone there)—is the only way to complete the picture, the only way to achieve an accurate framework for the dinosaur's shape and size.

With the *Brontosaurus* head, paleontologists used a skull for the composite that was not from the same species—thus opening up the reconstruction to possible mistakes. And without an accurately reconstructed skeleton, the fleshed-out image created by the artist essentially becomes an exercise in make-believe.

"Not only does the skeleton establish the animal's overall dimensions," explains Mark Hallett. *"It can also indicate posture, musculature, and possible habits."*

Putting muscles—which are not preserved in the fossil record—on a long-gone dinosaur seems like an impossible task. And paleoartists admit that determining muscle size is not an exact science. But having a keen sense of anatomy helps guide them, as do the fossil bones themselves, with their distinctive scars and ridges that indicate areas of muscle attachment.

Understanding how muscles function and comparing that knowledge to how scientists *think* a dinosaur might have behaved in its day-to-day life is especially helpful.

"It's very useful to work out what its lifestyle would be in order to put flesh on the bones," explains John Sibbick.

Mark Hallett adds: "It's very important to know the environment. The dinosaurs are products of their environments—they were constantly adapting to their environments. It's terribly important to look at lifestyle."

Here, evidence uncovered by other scientists can also be invaluable to the artist. Geologists can determine the physical geography of the land those oh-so-many millions of years ago. Swamp land, savannah, dense forest, frozen tundra . . . paleoartists know that a dinosaur must be physically adapted to the land it inhabits.

By examining plant fossils, paleobotanists can identify many types of ancient plants and food sources that were available and then, in turn, how they might have affected dinosaur size, eating habits, and interaction.

© Greg Paul. This *Corythosaurus* lived in the late Cretaceous period in a habitat that was well watered and forested and that had coastal marshes and swamps. Greg Paul drew these images from a number of known complete skeletons and skulls, including a nearly complete mummy with the majority of its skin. The skeletons showed down-curved vertebrae that would support deep ligaments to the head and would lower the shoulders. This helped inform the musculature study. Also helpful was knowledge of its habitat (through geologic/rock fossils) and the fact that this dinosaur was a plant-eating herbivore, known from the grinding patterns on teeth fossils.

All of that evidence combined with bones, bones, and more bones helps tease out a more complete picture of the dinosaurs' lifestyles—and thus, a better understanding of dinosaurs themselves.

ONE FROZEN EXPRESSION OR POSE

"**Y**OU'VE GOT ONE CHANCE TO *sum up everything that's known about that dinosaur, in one moment of time—one frozen expression or pose,*" explains distinguished paleoartist Tyler Keillor.

To sum everything up—to visually define that dinosaur—paleoartists often turn to the skull itself . . . the head of the beast. And oh, what a crown jewel that head is: such a powerful jaw, such enormous teeth, such fierce eyes!

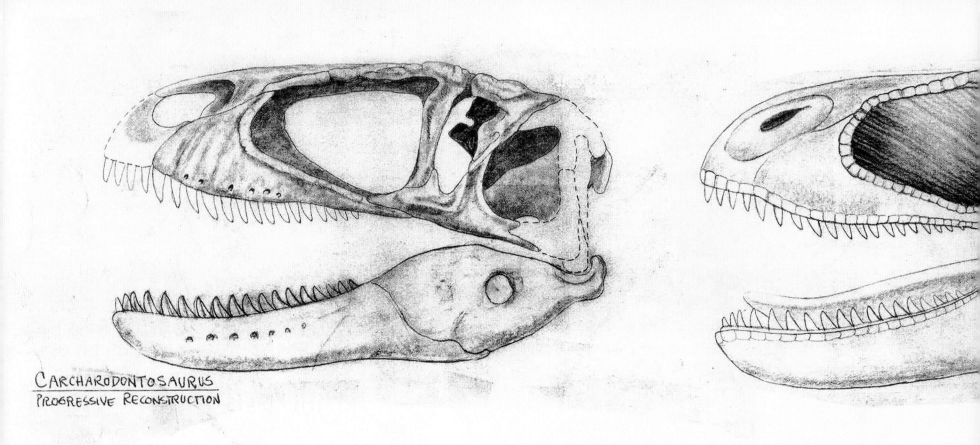

CARCHARODONTOSAURUS
PROGRESSIVE RECONSTRUCTION

As with the skeleton, getting the skull reconstruction right is critical to the accuracy of the overall appearance. But mistakes can, and do, happen.

The *Carcharodontosaurus* lost its distinction of Longest Skull of the Theropods when scientists discovered that they had misinterpreted the size of the original skull (the type specimen)—which was missing several defining bones. Later discoveries would show a skull length of only five feet rather than six. (Still awfully big, and still bigger than *T. rex*'s!)

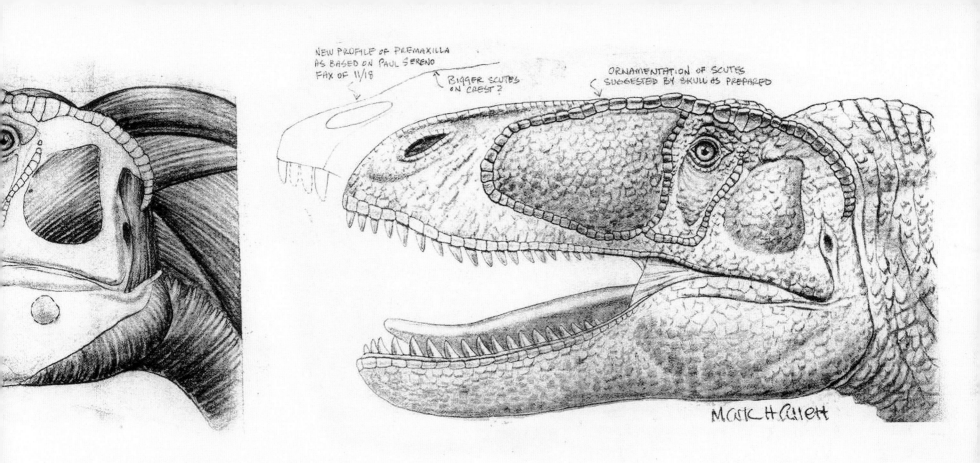

NEW PROFILE of PREMAXILLA
AS BASED ON PAUL SERENO
FAX OF 11/18

BIGGER SCUTES
ON CREST?

ORNAMENTATION OF SCUTES
SUGGESTED BY SKULL AS PREPARED

MARK Hallett

In addition to possible reconstruction snafus, with so many nitty-gritty details on the skull, it's hard to see how paleoartists can do a restoration with any degree of confidence. But luckily, the dinosaur's own anatomy simplifies things. Because it turns out dinosaurs had no facial muscles.

As with their bird and reptile relatives, dinosaur skin lies directly atop the bone. From the artist's perspective, this is a good thing. A lack of muscle makes restoring the skull (at least part of it) more of a known quantity.

© Mark Hallett. The original *Carcharodontosaurus* skull found in Africa was missing the premaxilla (upper cranial bones on the tip of upper jaw), which led to the misinterpretation of the skull's length. In Mark Hallett's sketch, he references a fax from paleontologist Paul Sereno, who discovered a fairly complete skull in Morocco with more accurate measurements. Hallett's study was based entirely on a photo and personal correspondence with Sereno. (See full restoration of this dinosaur on page 34.)

When they are predicting the unknown, paleoartists build on what they do know, relying on their skills in comparative anatomy—comparing an unknown dinosaur skull to known skulls of dinosaurs' living animal relatives (birds and reptiles) and to other dinosaur fossils.

"When we look at a dinosaur bone and see some of these same features that look identical to what we might see in an animal alive today, [we] can dissect and study the animal's skull," explains Keillor. *"Then [we] look at them side by side and [we] can kind of see what soft structures might be growing over what [we're] seeing on the dinosaur skull."*

In addition to soft structures, there are hard, bony elements known as skull adornments. These are the beastly frills found on ceratopsians like *Triceratops* that are weird and wild *and* found directly in the fossil record. Head frills and horns and spikes are bony structures that can be fossilized in the same way as the skull or skeleton bones are.

Of course, even those fossils can sometimes be misinterpreted. A preserved "horn" was found with the first *Iguanodon* (one of the first dinos ever discovered) and, as shown in the Waterhouse image, was placed on the creature's snout, like a rhinoceros's horn. Later *Iguanodon* discoveries would show that the nose horn was really a spike—and it belonged on the thumb!

© John Sibbick. This reconstruction of *Anchiceratops* was based on fossil material found in Alberta, Canada. A smaller ceratopsian than its famous relative *Triceratops*, *Anchiceratops* had an estimated body length of up to nineteen feet, with the enormous head frill taking up a large part of it. The forward-facing horns were the real weapons. Sibbick's reconstruction was an attempt to suggest that the large surface area of the skull could have used color and pattern to intimidate a predator or attract a mate. (See page 5 for another *Anchiceratops*.)

And what about expression? How is that determined? That outta-my-way-I'm-coming-through look; or that I-might-be-munching-on-leaves-but-I'll-crush-you-like-a-bug look? Unlike humans, who have over twenty different facial muscles to contort into unlimited expressions, dinosaurs had none. (But of course they had powerful jaw muscles!)

"The shape of the skull, the bone itself, gives the expression," says John Sibbick. *"The emphasis in* T. rex, *for example, is all around the mouth."*

Adds Greg Paul, *"If you have a predatory dinosaur attacking an herbivore, you're likely to show the mouth open—ready to attack. That's going to give a sense of expression."*

Knowing that predatory dinosaurs ate meat (i.e., other dinosaurs) informs the artist's decision to show this behavior in action. This sense of expression, this sense of energy—certainly in the skull, but also in the full-body skeleton—not only perfectly sums up the lifestyle of the dinosaur, but also truly helps to bring the dinosaur to life.

© Mark Hallett. The artist shows an adult *Carcharodontosaurus* defending its kill from *Deltadromaeus*. Hallett was able to draw on several partial skulls and parts of a skeleton to flesh out this dinosaur. The skull reflects the known skull dimensions gathered from Sereno's discovery. (See skull sketches on pages 30–31.)

THEY GET VERY ORNAMENTAL

Though skin is a soft tissue that naturally rots away with time, it sometimes leaves an impression in the soft mud and sediment, which can in turn become fossilized.

The first patch of dinosaur skin was discovered early on (in 1852) and clearly showed a unique scale pattern. Unfortunately, the animal it came from (*Pelorosaurus*) wasn't yet recognized as a dinosaur—it was briefly thought to be a giant crocodilian!

As the years ticked by, scientists continued to find more and more of these fossilized skin impressions—from all types of dinosaurs: theropods, sauropods, ceratopsians, ornithopods, and stegosaurs.

"The skin of dinosaurs, based on what we have found, is scaly, but it's a rounded scale that forms a rosette type pattern," explains renowned paleoartist Stephen Czerkas. *"They get very ornamental."*

The best-known skin impressions (well-preserved large quantities) come from the duck-billed dinosaurs, the hadrosaurs.

© Greg Paul. The artist's restoration of *Triceratops* in a bog. The large, conical scales are based on recently found fossil skin. No other known ceratopsid has the conical scales; all of the others have the flat scales. (See pages 13 and 20–21 for additional *Triceratops* and page 24 for skeletal mount.)

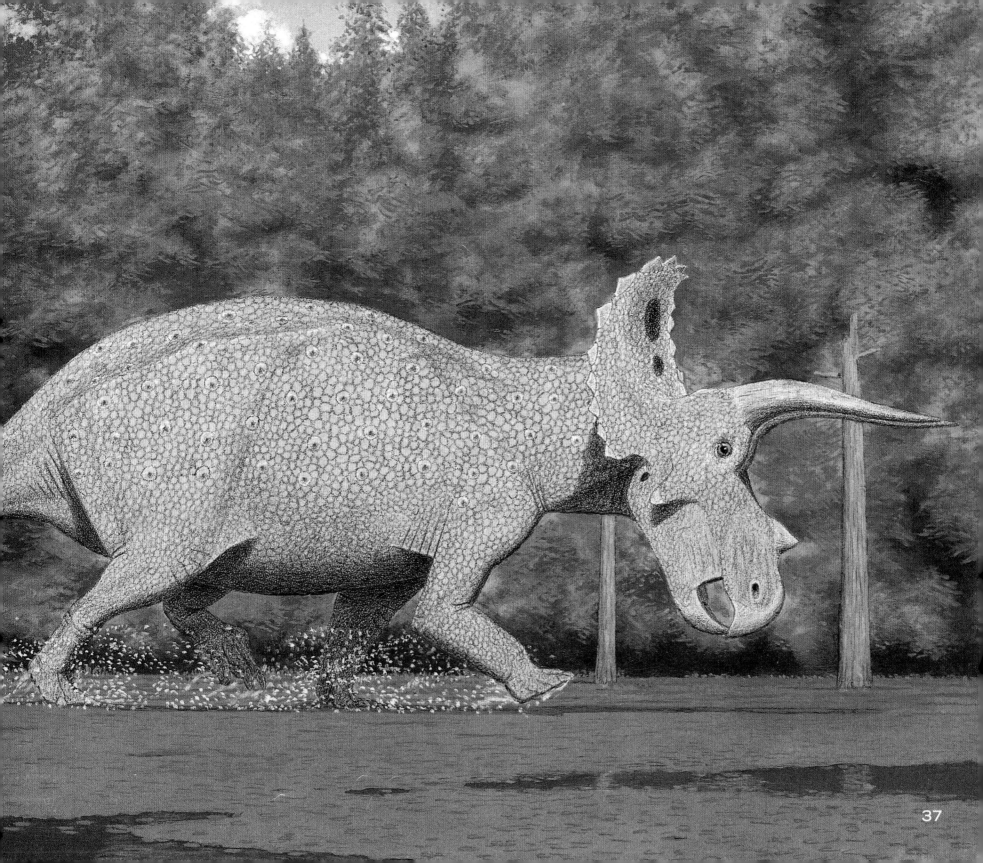

"But the most spectacular dinosaur scales known adorn Triceratops," *asserts Greg Paul. "Some scales were as big as the palm of your hand."*

Not only have scientists discovered a relatively large number of skin impressions, but they have uncovered some dinosaur mummies as well. Dino mummies present a fossilized framework of the soft organic tissues of not just skin, but ligaments and tendons, too—and it comes from most of the animal's body, not just an isolated portion.

Working from what is known of the scales (semi-hexagonal in shape, rosette pattern) toward what is unknown (how the scales were distributed over the entire body), the paleoartists often make comparisons to modern analogs—that is, to living animals such as a Jackson's chameleon or a Komodo dragon.

These comparisons help give them a better idea of how the scales might be arranged on a living creature. For example, an artist might put smaller scales on areas that require flexibility, such as knees and ankles, but a broader pattern of larger scales on other areas that don't flex.

"There are certain things you can and can't do with dinosaurs," explains Greg Paul. "For example, lizards and snakes have overlapping scales, but no dinosaur has those. So if you put overlapping scales on dinosaurs, you're being very inappropriate."

But just as scientists and paleoartists were feeling more confident about their understanding of dinosaur skin, something else came along and changed the view completely . . . dino feathers.

LEFT: Komodo dragon © Corbis.
RIGHT: Jackson's chameleon © Corbis.
Though a Komodo dragon is not a particularly close relative of the dinosaurs, it is helpful to some artists to study the largest known reptile for insights into how skin might cover a large animal and how it might move and be colored and present in different patterns at different places. A Jackson's chameleon is useful for the same reasons, but also it is the only known living animal with three horns atop its head—just like the dinosaur *Triceratops*!

Many scientists have long thought that birds and dinosaurs were related because they share a number of unique skeletal features (as well as many other similarities). If this relationship was true, scientists argued, some dinosaurs *must* have been feathered.

Then one day in 1996, in China, paleontologists unearthed a chicken-sized theropod—*Sinosauropteryx.* They found it with well-preserved, feather-like impressions outlining its entire body. And—boom!—the decades-long debate (did they have feathers or didn't they?) exploded.

Based on that remarkable first find, as well as several other extraordinary discoveries of feathered species, paleoartists had to reexamine the appearance of several well-established dinosaurs—particularly close relatives of these new feathered finds.

Stephen and Sylvia Czerkas's extraordinary life-sized reconstruction of the dinosaur *Deinonychus*—which served as the model for the raptors in the *Jurassic Park* movies—fell victim to the new evidence.

"We spent three years working on the Deinonychus *models," explained Sylvia. "Every single scale was delineated. It took forever to do those scales. But as the science marched on, and when it was eventually realized that this type of animal had feathers . . . well, we had new scientific information now and we were convinced that they had to have feathers."*

© Stephen and Sylvia Czerkas.
Deinonychus was, relatively speaking, fairly new to science and, due to its clawed foot (pages 14, 15), was terribly important, as it would change how people thought about dinosaurs. This sculpture reflected the most current information about the dinosaurs, including what was known about dinosaur skin.

40

Stephen adds: "But that's what you have to do. You have to be ready to

change what you think in the face of new scientific evidence . . . When we first did Deinonychus, *and at the time of* Jurassic Park, *feathers were unknown for any kind of dinosaur. But now the evidence is undeniably clear that* Deinonychus *and many types of dinosaurs were feathered."*

So now that dinosaurs are known to have been covered in either feathers or non-overlapping scaly skin, a more detailed image emerges—albeit still sprinkled with speculation. But that image begs another question: Were those details green, gray, or brightly patterned?

In 2000, *Deinonychus* got a makeover. New discoveries of smaller feathered dromaeosaurus (the family *Deinonychus* belongs to) made it necessary to rethink *Deinonychus*, whose skeletal anatomy was very similar to the feathered dinosaurs in its family. (See page 14 for skeletal mount.)

COLOR IS A REAL PROBLEM

"*THE COLOR IS MUCH MORE speculative than the skin texture or the feathers,*" explains Sylvia Czerkas, "*because we have so much fossil evidence that shows us what the structure of the skin was like and what the feathers looked like. There's much less imagination or speculation that goes into the skin textures. Whereas, with the color, that remains much more open to speculation.*"

It's the question most often asked of paleoartists: How do you know what color the dinosaurs were? And the paleoartists' response? *It is a problem.*

For an artist, dinosaur coloring is based first on the assumption, and the likely probability, that dinosaurs had color vision. This assumption is based on the current understanding of evolution, the biochemistry of color vision (how the cones in the retina perceive color in light), and the fact that both birds and reptiles (dinosaurs' closest relatives) can see a wide spectrum of colors.

"*I try to come up with a coloration that's grounded in nature,*" explains Tyler Keillor, "*so it doesn't look too exotic or doesn't look like science fiction—doesn't look like an alien—but looks like a real animal you might encounter . . . at a zoo or something.*"

© Tyler Keillor. The artist based this life-sized bust of *Herrerasaurus* upon a well-known and well-preserved fossil skull. The skin and the scale pattern were inspired by Komodo dragons (the largest living lizards). No fossil skin impressions of *Herrerasaurus* are known to exist to confirm or refute the artist's choice. (Though new feathered finds may affect the future look of this dinosaur too!) (See page 39 for Komodo dragon.)

If dinosaurs could, in fact, see the full color spectrum, it makes sense that their outer covering would have been made up of most color possibilities: colors they would have used to blend in to their environment, or to recognize herd members, or for display purposes, including to attract a mate.

"Color is a real problem," concedes John Sibbick. *"The* Parasaurolophus *series I did was an exercise in telling people it's a guess."*

© John Sibbick. Sibbick shows the tricky decisions involved when restoring dinosaurs, particularly with regard to color and pattern in this *Parasaurolophus* series. The artist chose three pattern types to highlight (from left to right): display, disruptive, and camouflage. This dinosaur grew fairly large (up to twenty-nine feet) and had a large surface area to disguise or enhance.

"You are choosing your colors based on modern analogs: the vegetarian, the meat-eater, the desert-dweller, the forested creature. It's easier for me to reconstruct the dinosaur and then tone everything down."

Greg Paul adds: "Except for the improbability of gaudy colors like pink and purple, any pattern is both speculative and possible."

A display pattern might be needed by an animal to enhance its "threatening" look to potential predators, or could be used to attract a mate. Disruptive patterns would break up the body outline (particularly in a desert or plains type of environment) and make it easier for herd members to find each other. Camouflage patterns work to hide an animal in its environment (to avoid predators).

45

Many scientists and artists speculate that scales on the bigger dinosaurs were more suited to carrying bold colors similar to those of a giraffe or tiger rather than a duller color like that of elephant skin. Smaller dinosaurs—and particularly those with feathers—would be the best candidates for even more brightly colored patterns like birds and some reptiles.

"The problem paleoartists always face," says Stephen Czerkas, *"is should they be conservative while keeping it natural-looking and not doing anything that's too distracting, or should imagination run wild with vibrant colors by making comparisons with animals that are much more ornate and colorful?"*

Some of these problems may very well be in the early stages of resolution. It turns out that *Sinosauropteryx* was not content with turning the paleontological world upside down by proving that some dinosaurs had feathers—oh, no. *Sinosauropteryx* also had to offer up color. Actual, honest-to-goodness pigmentation in the tail feathers.

Scientists identified this color by putting the dino feathers under a powerful electron microscope and looking for pigment-carrying structures called melanosomes, present in modern-day animals and particularly in bird feathers. *Sinosauropteryx* had loads of them!

© Stephen Czerkas. *Sinosauropteryx* was the first dinosaur discovered with primitive feathers. It did not have the skeletal adaptations necessary for flight, but the feathers suggest the evolutionary connection to birds. The specific melanosomes found in *Sinosauropteryx*'s tail feathers revealed a reddish-brown striped pattern to the tail. So far, though, only the tail feathers have had color clearly identified.

For many years, the answer has always been that we would never know about color—it just doesn't get preserved in fossils," says Stephen Czerkas. "Well, with the advent of new technologies and new ways of analyzing things . . . now we're not so sure that we'll never know. . . . And if anything, I think we probably will know what kinds of colors were on certain kinds of dinosaurs."

After a hundred-plus years of dino color being a problem, paleoartists are slowly starting to find some answers. And years from now . . . ?

What will we see?

THERE'S ONLY PROBABILITY

"**U**SUALLY WITH A DINOSAUR YOU'VE got gaps in the data; you've got skeletons that are incomplete," says Tyler Keillor. "Or even if you've got a complete skeleton, you likely don't have skin impressions to let you know the details of what the flesh looked like. . . . Or maybe you do have skin impressions, but they're from only part of the body and not the whole body."

Reconstructing a dinosaur . . . bringing it back to life (well, minus the actual breathing and terrorizing part) is a step-by-step-by-step process: working from the inside out—bones, muscles, skin, feathers, color.

No detail is too small for the paleoartist to gather. For example, digging through fossilized dino poop and examining teeth can distinguish the meat-eaters from the plant-eaters. Examining bone scars can reveal injuries and indicate which dinosaurs battled against each other. Each nugget of information helps inform the final dinosaur portrait.

Still, a question remains.

© Stephen Czerkas. This *Tyrannosaurus rex* (*T. rex*) reflects what is currently known about both the skeletal anatomy and the scaly skin, based on known skin impressions (more than thirty skeletons of *T. rex* have been discovered). Recently, though, relatives of *T. rex* have been found with primitive feathers, which may mean *T. rex* had some type of feathery covering as well. (See pages 3, 13, 50, and 53 for additional *T. rex* images.)

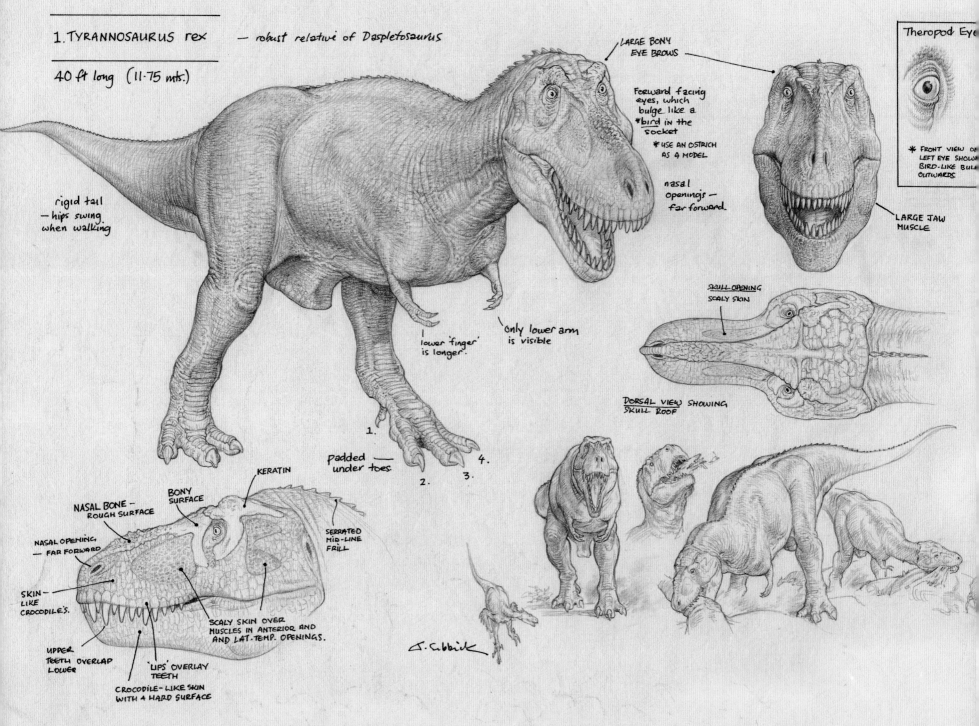

1. TYRANNOSAURUS rex — robust relative of Daspletosaurus

40 ft long (11·75 mts.)

rigid tail
— hips swing
when walking

LARGE BONY
EYE BROWS

Forward facing
eyes, which
bulge like a
*bird in the
socket
*USE AN OSTRICH
AS A MODEL

nasal
openings —
far forward.

Theropod Eye

* FRONT VIEW OF
LEFT EYE SHOWING
BIRD-LIKE BULGE
OUTWARDS.

LARGE JAW
MUSCLE

SKULL OPENING
SCALY SKIN

DORSAL VIEW SHOWING
SKULL ROOF

lower 'finger'
is longer.

Only lower arm
is visible

1.

2.   3.   4.

padded
under toes.

KERATIN

BONY
SURFACE

NASAL BONE —
ROUGH SURFACE

SERRATED
MID-LINE
FRILL

NASAL OPENING
— FAR FORWARD

SKIN
LIKE
CROCODILE'S.

SCALY SKIN OVER
MUSCLES IN ANTERIOR AND
AND LAT. TEMP. OPENINGS.

UPPER
TEETH OVERLAP
LOWER

'LIPS' OVERLAY
TEETH

CROCODILE-LIKE SKIN
WITH A HARD SURFACE

J. Cibbick

50

How come Stephen's *T. rex* (on the previous page) looks different from John's *T. rex* (here), which is different from Greg's *T. rex* (on page 53) and also from Tyler's and from Mark's?

Generally, these expert artists have access to the same bones, the same research studies, the same photographs, the same scientific specialists. And yet, there are five fairly different-looking dinosaurs. Why?

Tyler Keillor sums it up this way: "I think in a way, the artist wants to do something different. They should really come up with a way to put their own stamp on this particular animal. And so I think that accounts for a lot of the differences you'll see. Even though we're all starting with the same framework, you have a certain range of artistic choices to make."

Years ago, there were fewer bones and fewer skulls and less skin and no color, and there were many more artistic choices that had to be made. Today, these choices are more limited for the paleoartists intent on scientific accuracy. As the evidence accumulates and changes—more bones and more skulls and more skin and some color . . . and trackways and nesting grounds, and technologies such as CT scans and electron microscopes—the artists must go where the science takes them.

© Natural History Museum, London. John Sibbick created this *T. rex* pencil sketch as part of a project for the Natural History Museum, London, in an effort to aid model makers working on full-scale animatronic dinosaurs for theme parks. The sketch shows multiple views along with written notes on ideas of mobility and behavior. (See pages 3, 13, 49, and 53.)

"Within reconstructions," says Keillor, "there are all sorts of moments in time in the life story of these dinosaurs that artists can capture. And really, they're all probably equally valid as long as they're not too speculative—as long as they're based on the science and based on some logical idea."

After looking through the fossil window—after sifting and sorting and studying the abundance of scientific evidence; after sprinkling in speculation to fill in the gaps—a *probable* image of the dinosaur finally emerges.

But still, somewhere out there, there is more evidence; there are more pieces of the puzzle—as yet undiscovered; as yet not fully understood. Something unheard of today might become known tomorrow; tomorrow's discoveries might upend what is known today.

So, if no one has ever seen a dinosaur before . . .
if no one has ever snapped a photo or painted a portrait or built a sculpture by observing one of these living, breathing beasts . . .
how do we know what they really looked like?

Most scientists and paleoartists agree with John Sibbick's assessment:

"There's only probability, really. . . . Unless we see one walking through the door . . ."

ABOUT THE ARTISTS

John Sibbick has been drawing dinosaurs since he was twelve years old. He attended a four-year art college in England and worked in three design studios doing graphic design and illustration before becoming a freelance illustrator. His work can be seen in numerous books (including some children's reference books) and several different museums, including the Natural History Museum in London. FUN FACT: John has an ornithocheirid pterosaur named after him—*Ludodactylus sibbicki*!

WWW.JOHNSIBBICK.COM

Greg Paul is largely self-taught as an artist. He studied oils in college, and studied dinosaurology informally at Johns Hopkins before getting his first professional work at age twenty-two—though he's

been interested in dinosaurs and paleoart for as long as he can remember. His work can be seen in numerous books, magazines, museum exhibits, and commercial products. FUN FACT: Greg did more than any other artist to set the "new" look of the dinosaurs based on the dino revolution of the 1970s.

WWW.GSPAULDINO.COM

Since 1974, **Mark Hallett** has expressed his passion for prehistoric creatures by specializing as a paleoartist. His work has appeared in *Life, Smithsonian, National Geographic,* and many other scientific journals and popular books. In 1986, his paintings toured museums around the world, including the Smithsonian Institution's National Museum of Natural History and the American Museum of Natural History. Some of these exhibits opened other doors: Mark was chosen as an artistic consultant by Steven Spielberg to help create the dinosaurs of *Jurassic Park,* and later created many of the scenes and leading dinosaur characters for Disney Features' epic film *Dinosaur!.* FUN FACT: Mark coined the term *paleoart* to refer to an illustrator who researches and recreates the life of the past based on evidence. **WWW.HALLETTPALEOART.COM**

Tyler Keillor began drawing dinosaurs and monsters at age

four. He is largely self-taught as an artist and continues to experiment and learn to this day. He has been professionally preparing fossils, creating skeletal reconstructions, and sculpting flesh models of prehistoric life at the University of Chicago since 2001. His work can be seen in more than twenty-five museums around the world, including Chicago's Field Museum and the Natural History Museum of Vienna. FUN FACT: Some of Tyler's artistic skills were honed working as an assistant creating special effects and makeup for film, TV, and theater.

WWW.TYLERKEILLOR.COM

Sylvia Czerkas has had an interest in art and in animals ever since she was a child. As a teenager, she taught herself sculpting, then went on to college to major in art and exhibit her work in galleries and museums. While researching the

work of Charles Knight, she became interested in dinosaurs. For the last thirty years, she and her husband, Stephen, have been making life-sized dinosaurs, writing books, and organizing traveling museum exhibitions. In 1992, they founded The Dinosaur Museum in Blanding, Utah, where their sculptures and exhibits are on view. FUN FACT: Sylvia organized the first major paleoart exhibition.

WWW.DINOSAUR-MUSEUM.ORG

When he was about five years old, dinosaurs in motion pictures (like *King Kong*) had a strong influence on **Stephen Czerkas** and led him to a career in stop-motion animation, and making movies such as *Planet of Dinosaurs.* Later, along with his wife, Sylvia, he took his interests in dinosaurs in a more scientific direction and published several works on what dinosaurs looked like. Though he is self-taught as an artist and as a paleontologist, both he and Sylvia have received honorary doctorates for the paleo-work they have done. FUN FACT: Stephen's discovery put the spikes along the backs of sauropods, like *Diplodocus*.

WWW.DINOSAUR-MUSEUM.ORG

ACKNOWLEDGMENTS

The author wishes to thank and greatly acknowledge the following: John Sibbick, Tyler Keillor, Greg Paul, Mark Hallett, Sylvia Czerkas, and Stephen Czerkas; editor extraordinaire Ann Rider, editorial assistant Christine Krones, and designer Rachel Newborn; Mike Fredericks of *Prehistoric Times*; Juliet McConnell, Natural History Museum, London; Thomas Jorstad, Smithsonian Institution (NMNH); and Alex Navissi, American Museum of Natural History.

SELECTED SOURCES

Quoted sources are from tape-recorded interviews with the following in 2011–12: John Sibbick, Tyler Keillor, Greg Paul, Mark Hallett, Sylvia Czerkas, and Stephen Czerkas.

Bakker, Robert T. "Dinosaur Renaissance." *Scientific American.* April 1975, 58–78.

Czerkas, Sylvia J., and Everett C. Olson, editors. *Dinosaurs Past and Present,* vols. 1–2. Seattle: Natural History Museum of Los Angeles County in association with University of Washington Press, 1987.

Debus, Allen A., and Diane E. Debus. *Paleoimagery: The Evolution of Dinosaurs in Art.* Jefferson, N.C.: McFarland & Company, 2002.

Paul, Gregory S. *The Princeton Field Guide to Dinosaurs.* Princeton: Princeton University Press, 2010.

———, editor. *The Scientific American Book of Dinosaurs.* New York: St. Martin's Press, 2000.

Prehistoric Times. Publisher and editor Mike Fredericks. Vol. 27 (Dec. 1997/Jan. 1998); vol. 32 (Oct./Nov. 1998); vol. 36 (June/July 1999); vol. 38 (Oct./Nov. 1999); vol. 41 (April/May 2000); vol. 45 (Dec. 2000/Jan. 2001); vol. 46 (Feb./March 2001); vol. 54 (June/July 2002); vol. 56 (Oct./Nov. 2002); vol. 75 (Dec./Jan. 2006); vol. 85 (Spring 2008).

Roach, John. "Do They Really Look Like That? The Science of Dino Art." *National Geographic News,* online. March 11, 2003.

Weed, William Speed. "What Did Dinosaurs Really Look Like?" *Discover Magazine,* online. Sept. 2000.

Zimmer, Carl. "Study Offers an Insight into Dinosaur Colors." *New York Times,* online. Jan. 27, 2010.

GLOSSARY

ANATOMY: the branch of biology concerned with the structure of living things.

CARNIVORE: an animal that eats meat. Dinosaurs are identified as carnivores by the fossil teeth (sharpness and serration), having been bipedal (walked on two legs), and stomach remains (bones in the stomach).

COLD-BLOODED: having a body temperature that is not internally regulated.

DINOSAUR MUMMY: a dinosaur fossil including soft tissues that can be comprised of skin, ligaments, tendons, muscles, organs. Dino mummies are not actual preserved flesh; the flesh has been replaced by minerals that have hardened into the precise form of the tissues.

ELECTRON MICROSCOPE: a powerful microscope used to study organisms at the molecular level.

EVOLUTION: the theory that all living plants and animals originated from other, preexisting types of plants and animals.

FOSSIL: something preserved, such as a skeleton or a leaf imprint, from a past geologic age in the rock or sedimentary layers.

bone (or occasionally soft tissue), leaving hardened rock in the precise shape of the original—including fine details.

HERBIVORE: an animal that eats plants. Dinosaurs are identified as herbivores based on several things: grinding patterns on fossil teeth; presence of cheek teeth; presence of beak; having been quadrapedal (walked on four legs); presence of rocks in the stomach.

MELANOSOMES: microscopic spheres that are loaded with pigment.

MUMMY: soft tissues like skin and organs that have been preserved by a chemical process.

PALEO: ancient.

PALEOART: art that is representative of prehistoric time periods.

PALEONTOLOGIST: a scientist who specializes in the study of prehistoric life forms.

PIGMENT: cell or tissue matter that produces color.

PREDATOR: an animal that preys on (and eats) other animals (*see* carnivore).

PROBABILITY: the chance or likelihood that something will happen, or the degree to which it is accurate.

SPECIES: a biological classification; generally accepted as organisms that interbreed and can produce fertile offspring. Most of the general public refer to dinosaurs by their family name or genus. (That is what is done throughout this book.) For example, there are three distinct species of *Triceratops* known, and two species of *Tyrannosaurus* identified (*T. rex* is one species of *Tyrannosaurus*).

SPECULATIVE: theoretical, rather than factually based.

WARM-BLOODED: having a body temperature that is regulated internally.

AWARD-WINNING BOOKS BY THE SIBERT MEDALIST CATHERINE THIMMESH

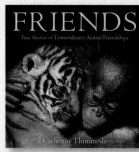
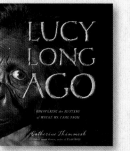

INDEX

Page numbers in **bold** refer to photos and illustrations.

MAJOR DINOSAUR GROUPS

THEROPODS

- small to ginormous in size

- most theropods were predatory/
  carnivores (ate meat; i.e., other
  dinosaurs)

- found on all continents

- found in Triassic, Jurassic, and
  Cretaceous periods

some examples of theropods (but not
limited to):

- *Rugops* - pp. 28, 29

- *Herrerasaurus* - p. 43

- *Megalosaurus*

- *Spinosaurus*

- *Allosaurus*

- *Carcharodontosaurus* - pp. 30, 31, 35

- *Albertosaurus* - p. 5

- *Daspletosaurus* - p. 19

- *Tyrannosaurus* - pp. 3, 13, 49, 50, 53

- *Sinosauropteryx* - p. 47

- *Deinonychus* - pp. 15, 40, 41

- *Velociraptor*

SAUROPODOMORPHS

- small to "colossal" in size

- herbivore (plant eating) and omnivore
  (plant, berry, meat eating)

- found on all continents

- found in Triassic, Jurassic, and
  Cretaceous periods

some examples of sauropodomorphs
(but not limited to):

- *Mamenchisaurus*

- *Apatosaurus (Brontosaurus)* - p. 23

- *Diplodocus*

- *Seismosaurus* - p. 6

- *Camarasaurus*

- *Brachiosaurus*

- *Giraffatitan*